WHAT IS WRONG WITH MARIJUANA?

50 QUESTIONS & ANSWERS

A **CHRISTIAN REFLECTION**
ON THE USE OF **MARIJUANA**

JESSE ROMERO, M.A.

mor
DEUS
PUBLISHING

What is Wrong with Marijuana?
50 Questions and Answers: A Christian
Reflection on the Use of Marijuana
Jesse Romero, M.A.

Cover image: Shutterstock.com
Cover and book design: Amor Deus Publishing Design Department

ISBN 978-1-61956-547-0

First Edition October 2016
10 9 8 7 6 5 4 3 2 1

Published and printed in the United States of America by Amor Deus Publishing, an imprint of Vesuvius Press Incorporated.

For additional inspirational books visit us at
AmorDeus.com

Here's a question for you: Would you smoke a joint with Jesus? Of course you wouldn't. Common sense and right reason tell you this. It's a no-brainer!

Yet there are many people today who do not use reason, lack common sense, and no longer think of Jesus. Trust me, I know. I was one of them.

Those familiar with my conversion story know that I was a total pothead during my youth and young adult years. For a decade of my life, I smoked weed just about every day. This behavior ultimately led me to drop out of high school, spend time in jail, get deported from a foreign country, and do two stints in drug rehabilitations centers. Smoking marijuana seriously messed up my life and created a nightmare for my family.

Although I was not raised in a Christian family, I did have many friends who were raised in a Christian household. Yet, like me, they, too, wanted to get high and feel good, justifying it by saying that their usage was not as extreme as mine since they only wanted to smoke marijuana recreationally. Over time, however, I witnessed *all* of them jettison their belief in Jesus and seek out a different belief system, one that condoned their recreational marijuana usage. They did this because nobody in their right mind believes that Jesus would condone smoking a joint.

Unfortunately, in order to justify their conscience, some of my friends became Rastafarians. I doubt any of them were informed that Bob Marley himself abandoned

Rastafarianism, surrendered his life to Jesus Christ, and asked to be baptized on his death bed! Yes, the King of Weed — who died of skin cancer at the age of 36 — was baptized a Christian on his deathbed and requested a Christian funeral service.

This is why *What is Wrong with Marijuana?* is such a needed book today. Jesse Romero, a Catholic Evangelist and retired Los Angeles Deputy Sheriff, presents us with the facts on marijuana, helping the people of today return to common sense, reason, and Jesus!

—Fr. Donald Calloway, MIC
Author of *No Turning Back: A Witness to Mercy*

Contents

I grew up, as a teenager in the 70's, was a young adult in the 80's. The drug culture (especially marijuana) was all around me, in my neighborhood, in the schools, amongst my family and friends. Today it is even more prevalent because it is legal in some states. President Obama has written about his many years of using marijuana. President Clinton says he would just hold marijuana joints to his mouth but never inhaled, really! These two presidents have broken the taboo of marijuana and have helped to normalize it in our libertine culture where everything is tolerated except Christian morality. This is a problem that is not going away. This is part of the culture of death, that is, the destruction of the human person through recreational intoxication. Marijuana usage is not deadly; I would call it *death by a thousand cuts.*

Secular humanist liberal progressives are more concerned about the pollution in the air; I am more concerned with the pollution of the soul. This book is a Catholic common-sense response to the marijuana culture that is being spawned and orchestrated by the Devil, the Father of Lies and the Deceiver. Catholic parents need to be armed with good solid responses when their kids ask, "Mom, Dad, what's wrong with pot?" Worse, when you walk into your teenager's room and find him smoking pot or selling it. Telling your teen, "You can't smoke pot because I said so" is a line of conversation that will never work! <u>A teenager's heart will not accept what their mind does not embrace.</u> The human person was made for truth, and once he/she hears the truth, he/she knows it; however, the human person that is intoxicated cannot hear the voice of truth.

This is precisely where demons attack us, that is, in the mind (cf. Acts 5:3; 2 Corinthians 11:3).

The devil tries to normalize SIN through the culture of death. There is a catchy song produced way back in 1978 called 'Mary Jane' sung by Rick James. When you listen to the song, it is so soothing. Heck, I always thought the song was about a girl called "Mary Jane". Then someone pointed out to me that the words are a reference to "Marijuana". You could see how the words could inspire, influence or normalize the use of marijuana upon a low information lukewarm faithless individual who simply follows his passions instead of reason.

The song is listed as one of the *50 Best Weed Songs*. Although the late punk-funker Rick James would go down in history as Black pop's most notorious cocaine cowboy—and comic fodder for Dave Chappelle—there's no denying the stone-cold genius behind "Mary Jane," a track that combined elements of rock, pop, and doo-wop. Working alongside underrated producer Art Stewart, who engineered and produced for such Motown luminaries as Marvin Gaye and Stevie Wonder, wild boy James' brilliant song about buds paved the way for a whole puff, puff, pass generation of hip-hop and soul heads including Cypress Hill, Snoop Dogg, and D'Angelo. While coke, a least for Rick, was an evil drug that contributed to his decline, the brother could always count on Mary Jane to turn him on "with her love" and take him to paradise. Without a doubt, many parents might have thought their kids were listening to a love song about "the girl next-door," but of course, it was all about getting lifted.[1]

---

1   Gonzales, Michael A. "The 50 Best Weed Songs - 14. Rick James, *Mary Jane*" (1978). *Complex*. Complex Media, Inc. n.d. Web. 18 July 2016.

A Christian Reflection
on the Use of Marijuana

What is marijuana?

Answer:

Marijuana is made from dried leaves of the Cannabis sativa plant.

> Marijuana is the most commonly used illicit drug in the United States. Its use is widespread among young people. According to a yearly survey of middle and high school students, rates of marijuana use have steadied in the past few years after several years of increase. However, the number of young people who believe marijuana use is risky is decreasing. Legalization of marijuana for medical use or adult recreational use in a growing number of states may affect these views.[1]

> Tetrahydrocannabinol (THC) is the psychoactive ingredient. Marijuana is a gateway drug, introducing teens to other abusive substances. THC impairs short-term memory and psychomotor functions (that is why it is called DOPE). It contains cancer-causing agents and is psychologically addictive.[2]

How do people use marijuana?

Answer:

People smoke marijuana in hand-rolled cigarettes (*joints*) or in pipes or water pipes (*bongs*). They also smoke it in *blunts,* which are emptied cigars that have been partly or completely refilled with marijuana. To avoid inhaling smoke, more people are using vaporizers. These devices pull the active ingredients (including THC) from the marijuana and collect their vapor in a storage unit. A person then inhales the vapor, not the smoke. Users can mix marijuana in food (*edibles*), such as brownies, cookies, or candy, or brew it as a tea. A newly popular method of use is smoking or eating different forms of THC-rich resins. Smoking THC-rich resins extracted from the marijuana plant is on the rise. Users call this practice *dabbing.* People are using various forms of these extracts such as:

- *hash oil* or *honey oil*—a gooey liquid

- *wax* or *budder*—a soft solid with a texture like lip balm

- *shatter*—a hard, amber-colored solid

These extracts can deliver extremely large amounts of THC to users, and their use has sent some people to the emergency room. Another danger is in preparing these extracts, which usually involves butane (lighter fluid). A number of people who have used butane to make extracts at home have caused fires and explosions and have been seriously burned.[3]

Dabbing is yet another growing trend. More people are using marijuana extracts that provide stronger doses, and therefore stronger effects, of THC. Higher THC levels may mean a greater risk for addiction if users are regularly exposing themselves to high doses.[4]

A kid asked me why is smoking pot wrong and where is that in the Bible?

Answer:

In the next couple of pages I will respond Biblically, catechetically, legally, statistically, scientifically, and finally, from common sense. Here is the short answer as to *why smoking marijuana is wrong.* Because, in a nutshell, it *alters your mind, alters your judgment and alters your ability to think clearly and soberly.*

Can you show me in the Bible that smoking marijuana is morally wrong?

Answer:

There is no Bible verse that specifically says, "smoking marijuana is wrong;" however, as Catholic Christians we are called to have the pure, sober, renewed mind of Jesus Christ.

- Romans 12:1-2 (NAB) "I urge you therefore, brothers, by the mercies of God, to offer your bodies as a living sacrifice, holy and pleasing to God, your spiritual worship. Do not conform yourselves to this age but <u>be transformed by the renewal of your mind</u>, that you may discern what is the will of God, what is good and pleasing and perfect."

- 1 Corinthians 2:16 (NAB) "For who has known the mind of the Lord, so as to counsel him?" But, <u>we have the mind of Christ</u>.

- 2 Corinthians 10:5 (NAB) and every pretension raising itself against the knowledge of God, and <u>take every thought captive in obedience to Christ</u>.

When you read the above three Bible verses it is clear that the Lord wants us to have transformed and renewed minds. My question is, "How can you have the pure holy mind of Jesus if you are under the influence of marijuana?" You can't!

Is there a specific Bible verse that condemns the recreational use of drugs for the purpose of altering the mind?

Answer:

Yes in…

- Galatians 5:19-20 (NAB) "Now the works of the flesh are obvious: immorality, impurity, licentiousness, idolatry, <u>sorcery</u>, hatreds, rivalry, jealousy, outbursts of fury, acts of selfishness, dissensions, factions, occasions of envy, drinking bouts, orgies, and the like. I warn you, as I warned you before, that those who do such things will not inherit the kingdom of God."

- Revelation 9:21 (NAB) "Nor did they repent of their murders, their <u>magic</u> potions, their unchastity, or their robberies." "Magic potions" were drugs in the ancient world.

- Revelation 18:23 (NAB) "No light from a lamp will ever be seen in you again. No voices of bride and groom will ever be heard in you again. Because your merchants were the great ones of the world, all nations were led astray by your <u>magic</u> potion." "Magic potions" were drugs in the ancient world.

- Revelation 22:14-15 (NAB) "Blessed are they who wash their robes so as to have the right to the tree of life and enter the city through its gates. Outside are the dogs, the <u>sorcerers</u>, the unchaste, the murderers, the idol-worshipers, and all who love and practice deceit."

You will notice that "sorcery" is condemned as work of the flesh and those who practice this will not get to heaven. It is interesting that the word "sorcery" in the two passages that I have cited above is translated as such from the Greek work *pharmakeia*. The word *pharmakeia* "primarily signified the use of medicine, drugs, spells, poisoning, and sorcery. In 'sorcery' the use of drugs, whether simple or potent, was generally accompanied by incantations and appeals to occult (demonic) powers."[5]

In other words, you can clearly see the direct connection in Sacred Scripture by the study of this word "sorcery". It was directly connected with the use of drugs, potions, and medicines to alter the mind of the user in order to engage in occult demonic practices. "Every pagan religion has had a drug rite ingrained somewhere in its ritualistic practice. Marijuana produces feelings of transcendence that may make users think they are <u>gods</u> or that they possess insights denied non-users…Satan, who disguises himself as an 'angel of light,' (2 Corinthians 11:14 NAB) uses drugs (in Greek: *pharmakeia*) to create the passive and spiritually open state of consciousness that leads to demonic influence"[6] such as infestation, obsession, oppression, and possession. Even simple "temptation which is common activity of the demons, and it is directed at all men" is virtually impossible to resist if you are not sober and your mind is altered. The devil wants to control your mind so that he can control your thoughts, emotions, behavior, destroy your soul and take you to HELL! "That is why he (Satan) tries to force man's body to become an occasion for sin. He tries to humiliate the body, to break it as a raging reaction against the incarnation of the Word"[7]

Does the Bible call us to live a life of sobriety?

Answer:

The Bible mentions that we should be "sober" at least six times in the New Testament:

- Acts 26:25 (RSV) But Paul said, "I am not mad, most excellent Festus, but I am speaking the <u>sober</u> truth."

- Romans 12:3 (NAB) For by the grace given to me, I tell everyone among you not to think of himself more highly than one ought to think, but to think <u>soberly</u>, each according to the measure of faith that God has apportioned.

- 1 Thessalonians 5:6 (NAB) Therefore, let us not sleep as the rest do, but let us stay alert and <u>sober</u>.

- 1 Peter 1:13 (NAB) Therefore, gird up the loins of your mind, live <u>soberly</u>, and set your hopes completely on the grace to be brought to you at the revelation of Jesus Christ.

- 1 Peter 4:7 (NAB) The end of all things is at hand. Therefore, be serious and <u>sober</u> for prayers.

- 1 Peter 5:8-9 (NAB) Be <u>sober</u> and vigilant. Your opponent the devil is prowling around like a roaring lion looking for someone to devour. Resist him, steadfast in faith…

What does "sober" mean?

Answer:

Sober is the Greek word, *sophron* (adjective) which means "of sound mind", "self-controlled" and "temperate." Sober used as a verb in Greek means "to be free from the influence of intoxicants" also "the cultivation of sound judgment and prudence." Used as an adverb, sober means "the exercise of self-restraint that governs all passions and desires enabling the believer to be conformed to the mind of Christ." The word sober in the Bible is also used in association with the word "watchfulness"[8] which is a military word used to remind someone to be prepared for battle. In other words, we are called to be prepared for spiritual warfare, and we can only do so if we are sober!

Is there a connection between sobriety and human rationality?

Answer:

Saint Thomas Aquinas and the Christian tradition identify man's rational intellect as what makes us "in the image of God." Humans use logic. We are rational. We have an intellect. Humans play chess. Humans follow the rules of grammar. Humans build suspension bridges. Humans paint images. Humans travel to the moon and back. Humans write novels. This is what makes humans like God and the angels. Our logical, rational intellect is the greatest gift that God granted our species. Judaism and Christianity, therefore, traditionally identify the blurring of this great gift (the intellect) as sinful. Being intoxicated with alcohol has always been condemned by Scripture and Tradition – going all the way back to Moses.[9]

Here's a sample:

"Now the works of the flesh are obvious: immorality, impurity, licentiousness, idolatry, sorcery, hatreds, rivalry, jealousy, outbursts of fury, acts of selfishness, dissensions, factions, occasions of envy, *drinking bouts*, orgies, and the like. I warn you, as I warned you before, that those who do such things will not inherit the kingdom of God" (cf. Galatians 5:19-21 (NAB)).

The New Testament lists *sins that prevent inheriting the kingdom of God,* historically identified as "mortal sins" by the Catholic Church. Drunkenness is evil because it blurs and muddies our highest faculty – rationality.

Think about it. When a person is drunk, he resorts to how animals act. Drunk people act irrationally. Drunk people do not use language properly. They do not think logically. Their moral compass fades. They sometimes fail to control their bodily functions. They cannot operate cars or machines because their intellect has lost its facility. The more drunk you become, the less human you act. By the way, this is how you know when you have crossed the line between being "merry of heart" and "drunk as a skunk." If you cannot perform rational tasks, you have crossed the line.[10]

Is there a connection between marijuana and rationality?

Answer:

I will show my cards up front. I was born in 1961 and I have never smoked marijuana. I do not know how it feels. Therefore, I do not write from experience; however, I am a retired Los Angeles Deputy Sheriff which makes me a trained observer. I have observed pot-smokers quite a bit. I have been to my fair share of concerts, parties, and sporting events.

> Marijuana…inhibits the intellect. It doesn't just provide a buzz (like drinking two beers). I grant that it may not be as bad as being stone cold drunk, but it's still a "high" that inhibits the intellect. From the point of view of Christian anthropology, it's a slam-dunk. Smoking marijuana is sinful to the extent that it inhibits the highest function of the soul. This would apply to cocaine, heroin, crystal meth, and other drugs.[11]

Saint Thomas Aquinas says regarding the theory of knowledge that *"what is received is received according to the mode of the receiver."*[12] Let me apply this to marijuana users, the information (data) they receive, read, or hear is not processed clearly because their intoxicated state does not allow them to have the intellectual and moral clarity to receive the information (whatever that may be).

Question 10:
Does marijuana have negative spiritual implications?

Answer:

The facts are that marijuana destroys the soul's faculties (which are the intellect and will), hence rendering them weak and impaired. One cannot live a life of holiness and be in a state of grace while using (smoking) marijuana. Drug usage alters the state of the mind and can invite demonic activity. It promotes the loss of control of the mind as well as denying God's will for us, that is, to be sober-minded.

Dominican priest, Father Juan José Gallego, an exorcist from the Archdiocese of Barcelona in Catalonia, Spain… also warned that…addictions are "a type of possession."[13]

Addictions are like parasites, they eat away at your faith and your relationships.

A priest (Jeremy Davies) of Westminster, the leading diocese of the Catholic Church of England and Wales states:

> The Church's writings on exorcism and demonic possession say that a person can be influenced or even possessed by demonic forces when they are 'hardened' in serious sin and the Church specifies that these include people who are involved in heavy drug use, violence and sexual perversions.[14]

Are drugs good or bad?

Answer:

We live in a time of pharmaceuticals, recreational drugs and hard-core narcotics, as well as medical drugs. Many pharmaceuticals, of course, save lives. They often appear nearly magical in what they can do. There seems to be a drug for everything, even problems that one would not think are connected to chemicals. In the U.S. alone, more than $250 billion is spent on pharmaceuticals each year. Our reliance on them is fantastic. The Mayo Clinic reports that seventy percent of Americans are on at least one prescription drug. Anti-depressants are rampant (eleven percent of Americans are on these). Advertisements on television give us a clear idea of both the commercial aspects and (with those disclaimers) the many side effects. There is good. There is bad. There is overuse. Like anything else, some of it may be from God, while other aspects of it can be from Darkness. It's a bit mysterious, how drugs, particularly those that affect the mind, have long been associated with sorcery.[15]

Question 12:

Is there a connection between drug intoxication & the Occult?

Answer:

Yes, the Spanish writer Carlos Castaneda, whose books give glowing tales of pharmacological indulgence through the sorcerer Don Juan, have provided a societal backdrop for drugs and Satanism. Castaneda is the author of: 1) *Journey to Ixtlan*, 2) *The Power of Silence* and 3) *The Fire Within*.[16] This author "idealizes black magic practices...spell casting. He points out that all such Occult procedures are possible under the influence of hallucinogenic drugs...Many teenagers have read his books and imitate Castaneda's fusion of the Occult and narcotics"[17] to their detriment.

The Greek word for "witchcraft" [in *Galatians*] is *pharmakeia*, from which we get the word *pharmacy*, the place where prescription drugs are available, notes an expert in deliverance, George Bloomer. "In ancient times the pharmacist was one who mixed potions and poisons with which to influence and kill people. Today, illegal drugs enslave us and make us dependent. They waste our lives and our money."[18]

> "Illegal drugs plague our neighborhoods and families, robbing us of the next generation. At the same time, we must realize that we are also the most medicated people on earth. Never have so many people used prescription drugs. We have drugs to bring us out of depression and drugs to calm our stress. Antidepressant drugs are prescribed almost automatically today.

Although in some cases prescription drugs are helpful in correcting chemical imbalances in the brain, which is not the only cause of depression. Depression also can be the result of <u>demonic influence</u>. Drugs may treat the symptoms, but they fail to address the source of the depression. It is comparable to seeing someone with an arrow stuck in his chest and handing him an aspirin instead of removing the arrow."[19]

Is it possible that a person's problems are actually spiritual and they are just being medicated? Does this medication simply mask any demonic influence?

Answer:

It seems the best approach to anything medical is to always pray first, follow good professional advice, and look chiefly for the origin of a problem; there are certainly times when the problem is spiritual. This can be true for any disease. Spiritual sources can exacerbate a weakness, work in tandem with a physical cause, or cause the physical aspect to begin with. The etiology is often a mystery.[20]

George Bloomer (expert on deliverance) says,

> Not all drug use is bad. When properly administered, it can bring about healing as God intended or help people to endure severe pain. While, in some cases, these prescription drugs can be helpful in correcting such things as chemical imbalances in the brain, there are other causes of depression. Depression also can be the result of demonic influence. In such cases, drugs may treat the symptoms, but they will never be able to address the spiritual source of the depression.[21]

The bottom line is remembering how many times the Lord cast out "unclean spirits" and "demons" before affecting a cure in the New Testament. There is also the man at the tombs in Gadarenes, whose mental illness was caused not by psychological forces or biochemistry but by a "legion" (of demons).[22]

Why do people use marijuana and other mind-altering drugs?

Answer:

In the last few decades, millions of people have turned to drugs because of their mind-altering effects. Drugs are extremely powerful hallucinogens that cause people to experience bizarre distortions of reality. The effects of these drugs are often described as out of body adventures, mystical "highs", and a psychedelic blurring of fantasy and reality. People who have these experiences find it difficult to return to the mundane life of the real world. They crave deeper thrills and higher "highs."[23]

The drug culture helps people escape the reality of this world momentarily with all its pressures, stress, deadlines, responsibility, anxiety and challenges. It provides a way of escaping reality if only for a short while.

Question 15:

Is there a connection between smoking marijuana and schizophrenia?

Answer:

One such harm to the common good would be the growing evidence of a significant and consistent relationship between marijuana use and the development of schizophrenia and related disorders. Schizophrenia is considered one of the most devastating mental illnesses, and those who suffer from it require frequent and protracted medical care in psychiatric wards. It frequently causes visual or auditory hallucinations, cognitive impairment and severe social withdrawal.[24]

Marijuana is considered to be a hallucinogen and recent studies done in the U.S., Sweden, New Zealand and Holland that spanned as much as 15 years, demonstrate a strong correlation between marijuana use in youth and the development of schizophrenia later in life. An article in the *British Journal of Psychiatry* concluded that marijuana is a "causal component," among others, in the development of schizophrenia and other psychotic disorders. Facts derived from these studies demonstrate that marijuana use precipitates schizophrenia or related psychotic disorders in the brains of people who are inherently vulnerable to psychosis. So this begs the question as to why eighteen states plus the District of Columbia, (with six more states pending), legalized "medical" marijuana? Somehow, medicine and law have become a matter of a public vote and not objective scientific data.[25]

Professor Colin Blakemore, chief of the Medical Research Council, who backed our original campaign for cannabis to be decriminalized, has also changed his mind. He said, "The link between cannabis and psychosis is quite clear now; it wasn't 10 years ago."[26] <u>Psychosis</u> is defined as "a mental disorder characterized by symptoms, such as delusions or hallucinations that indicate impaired contact with reality. A serious mental disorder (as schizophrenia) characterized by defective or a loss of contact with reality often with hallucinations or delusions."[27]

Many medical specialists agree that the debate has changed. Robin Murray, professor of psychiatry at London's Institute of Psychiatry, estimates that at least 25,000 of the 250,000 schizophrenics in the UK could have avoided the illness if they had not used cannabis.

> The number of people taking cannabis may not be rising, but what people are taking is much more powerful, so there is a question of whether a few years on we may see more people getting ill as a consequence of that.[28]

"Society has seriously underestimated how dangerous cannabis really is," said Professor Neil McKeganey, from Glasgow University's Centre for Drug Misuse Research. "We could well see over the next 10 years increasing numbers of young people in serious difficulties."[29]

Mark Winstanley, of the charity Rethink Mental Illness, said, "Too often cannabis is wrongly seen as a safe drug, but as this review shows, there is a clear link with psychosis and schizophrenia, especially for teenagers."[30]

Question 16:

Does marijuana actually affect the brain or is that simply a religious urban legend?

Answer:

Long-term *marijuana* use may actually shrink certain parts of the *brain* and have lasting effects on mental health. A new study shows heavy marijuana use over several years was associated with structural differences in at least two different regions of the *brain*, the hippocampus and amygdala. Researchers found that the hippocampus, which is thought to regulate memory, was an average of 12% smaller among marijuana users, compared with people who did not smoke pot. The amygdala, involved in emotion and memory, was an average of 7% smaller.[31]

The study also suggests that long-term marijuana users were more likely to report symptoms associated with mental disorders...growing literature suggests that long-term cannabis use is associated with a wide range of adverse health consequences. In the study, researchers used high-resolution *magnetic resonance imaging* to compare the *brain* structure of 15 men who smoked more than five joints of marijuana daily for more than 10 years with images from 16 men who did not smoke pot. The participants also took a verbal memory test and were evaluated for symptoms of mental disorders. The results showed men who smoked pot regularly had significantly lower brain tissue volumes in the hippocampus and amygdala areas, as well as more symptoms of mental disorders... "There is ongoing controversy concerning the long-term effects of cannabis on the brain," write the researchers. "Although modest use may not lead to significant neurotoxic effects, these results suggest that heavy daily use might indeed be toxic to human brain tissue."[32]

What are the other health effects of marijuana?

Answer:

Marijuana use may have a wide range of effects, both physical and mental.

Physical effects: 1] *Breathing problems.* Marijuana smoke irritates the lungs, and frequent marijuana smokers can have the same breathing problems that tobacco smokers have. These problems include daily cough and phlegm, more frequent lung illnesses, and a higher risk of lung infections. Researchers still do not know whether marijuana smokers have a higher risk for lung cancer. 2] *Increased heart rate.* Marijuana raises heart rate for up to 3 hours after smoking. This effect may increase the chance of heart attack. Older people and those with heart problems may be at higher risk.[33]

Mental effects: 1] Long-term marijuana use has been linked to mental illness in some users, such as:

- Temporary *hallucinations*—sensations and images that seem real though they are not.

- Temporary *paranoia*—extreme and unreasonable distrust of others.

- Worsening symptoms in patients with *schizophrenia* (a severe mental disorder with symptoms such as hallucinations, paranoia, and disorganized thinking).

2] Marijuana use has also been linked to other mental health problems, such as depression, anxiety, and suicidal thoughts among teens. However, study findings have been mixed.[34]

What are the short and long-term effects of marijuana on the brain?

Answer:

Marijuana has both short- and long-term effects on the brain.

Short-term effects: When a person smokes marijuana, THC quickly passes from the lungs into the bloodstream. The blood carries the chemical to the brain and other organs throughout the body. The body absorbs THC more slowly when the person eats or drinks it. In that case, the user generally feels the effects after 30 minutes to one hour. THC acts on specific brain cell receptors that ordinarily react to natural THC-like chemicals in the brain. These natural chemicals play a role in normal brain development and function. Marijuana over activates parts of the brain that contain the highest number of these receptors. This causes the "high" that users feel. Other effects include:

— altered senses (for example, seeing brighter colors)

— altered sense of time

— changes in mood

— impaired body movement

— difficulty with thinking and problem-solving

— impaired memory[35]

Long-term effects: Marijuana also affects brain development. When marijuana users begin using as teenagers, the drug may reduce thinking, memory, and learning functions and affect how the brain builds connections between the areas necessary for these functions. Marijuana's effects on these abilities may last a long time or even be permanent. For example, a study showed that people who started smoking marijuana heavily in their teens and had an ongoing cannabis use disorder, lost an average of eight IQ points between ages 13 and 38. The lost mental abilities did not fully return in those who quit marijuana as adults. Those who started smoking marijuana as adults did not show notable IQ declines.[36]

NIDA Director Dora D. Volkow, M.D. said,

> THC...in marijuana, alters the ability of the hippocampus, a brain area related to learning and memory, to communicate effectively with other brain regions. In addition, we know from recent research that marijuana use that begins during adolescence can lower IQ and impair other measures of mental function into adulthood.[37]

How can you tell if a teenager has been using marijuana?

Answer:

Parents should be aware of the child's behavior, such as carelessness with grooming, mood changes, and deteriorating relations with family members and friends. In addition, changes in academic performance, increased absenteeism or truancy, lost interest in sports or other favorite activities, and changes in eating or sleeping habits could all be related to drug use or may indicate other problems. If someone is high on marijuana, he or she might:

- seem dizzy or uncoordinated
- seem silly and giggly for no reason
- have very red bloodshot eyes
- have a hard time remembering things that just happened
- be in possession of drugs and drug paraphernalia, including pipes and rolling papers
- have an odor on clothes and in the bedroom
- use incense and other deodorizers
- use eye drops excessively
- wear clothing or jewelry or have posters that promote drug use
- have unexplained use of money[38]

Question 20:

How can a simple green plant like marijuana cause any evil?

Answer:

Fr. Basil Nortz, ORC writes:

> With regard to plants…the devil may work through them to create disturbances around them. This form of infestation is sometimes the consequence of the place or the object being used for Satanic rituals or Occult practices, or because a curse or spell has been placed on them.[39]

It is common knowledge among narcotics officers in law enforcement that the Mexican and Columbian cartels call upon demons to curse, put spells, hexes and diabolical incantations on the drugs they manufacture and export. Most, if not all of the Drug Cartel members openly worship the devil. The drug cartels have an official religion called "La Santa Muerte" (Holy Death) which, according to the Catholic Bishops of Latin America, have universally stated that this perfidious figure is Satan himself. "The narcotics industry is…enormous. It funds terrorism and — this is a huge problem in America — it fuels the foreign gangs."[40]

I would recommend the book called *Coming Clean* by Dr Jorge Valdez. He was involved with the mass distribution of drugs for the Columbian Cartel. He openly speaks about the dark demonic side that under girds this illegal evil business. You can order it on the Internet.

What does the Catholic Church teach about recreational drugs that alter your mind?

Answer:

The Catechism of the Catholic Church teaches (paragraph 2291): "The use of drugs inflicts very grave damage on human health and life…They constitute direct co-operation in evil, since they encourage people to practices gravely contrary to the moral law." The Bible says "Thou Shall Not Kill" and using illegal drugs is a slow death. You are destroying your body cell by cell and your body is a temple of the Holy Spirit.[41]

Can smoking marijuana become habit-forming? Can it shape your character?

Answer:

The poet Samuel Smiles says: "Sow a thought, reap an act. Sow an act, reap a habit. Sow a habit, reap a character. Sow a character, reap a destiny."[42]

Why are recreational drugs immoral?

Answer:

Here is why drugs are immoral. Taking recreational (as opposed to therapeutic) drugs is intrinsically wrong. The *Charter for Health Care Workers* states: "using drugs is always illicit, because it implies an unjustified and irrational refusal to think, will and act as free persons."[43]

Recreational drugs are designed for the sole purpose of impairing our reason and our will, the very faculties made in God's image. While drug use is *objectively* wrong, a drug user might be subjectively less guilty because of the addiction drugs cause. In love, we should seek to free the person from this heavy bondage.[44]

Can you take mind-altering drugs and still follow the Lord and do God's will?

Answer:

No, Satan and Satanism is all about doing it YOUR WAY instead of GOD'S WAY. The <u>Church of Satan</u> founder <u>Anton LaVey</u> (1930-1997) taught his followers that they were their own gods and goddesses, their own final authority.[45]

Aleister Crowley was a famous European Satanist, Occultist, drug abuser, bisexual and a hedonist. In fact, he is the founder of Satanism in Europe. His mother called him "The Beast". The European press at the time called him "the wickedest man in the world." <u>Aleister Crowley</u> (1875-1947) wrote in his infamous *Book of the Law*, "Do What Thou Wilt Shall Be the Whole of the Law."[46]

In Hell, the damned sing in torment "I did it my way;" in Heaven, the saints sing joyfully, "I did it His way." (*"His" refers to Jesus Christ*).

Does the Bible warn us about simply following "our own way?"

Answer:

Yes...

- Proverbs 14:14 (RSV) A perverse man will be filled with fruit of his own ways...

- Proverbs 14:14 (Douay Rheims). A fool shall be filled with his own ways...

- Matthew 6:9-10 (NAB) "This is how you are to pray: Our Father in heaven, hallowed be your name, your kingdom come, Your will be done..."

- Proverbs 3:5-7 (NAB) "Trust in the LORD with all your heart, on your own intelligence do not rely. In all your ways be mindful of him, and he will make straight your paths. Do not be wise in your own eyes, fear the LORD and turn away from evil."

Marijuana makes you lose your free will.

Satanists use drug rituals during the practice of their religion. Why is that?

Answer:

The Satanic Bible has nines Satanic statements.[47] Here are numbers 1, 7, and 9. These Satanic precepts are easier to practice if the member is under the influence of drugs:

1. Satan represents indulgence, instead of abstinence.[48]

7. Satan represents man as just another animal, sometimes better, more often worse than those that walk on all fours, who, because of his "divine spiritual and intellectual development;" has become the most vicious of all animals.[49]

9. Satan represents all of the so-called sins, as they all lead to physical, mental or emotional gratification.[50]

Illegal drugs have destroyed so many people's lives, rich and poor alike. Who is behind the destructive drug culture?

Answer:

Satan is the CEO of this illegal destructive drug culture. Satan is *Abaddon* (in Hebrew) which means "the destroyer" – (Revelation 9:11). Satan is *Apollyon* (in Greek) which means "the destroyer" – (Revelation 9:11). This is how Satan is destroying our society and creating a culture of death, in part through our fascination with drugs and intoxication. Our Lord Jesus Christ described Satan as a liar and a murderer from the very beginning. (cf. John 8:44)

Question 28:

Is marijuana sinful?

Answer:

Does smoking marijuana count as a sin? As you know, marijuana is becoming legal in certain states. So once again, the ethics of marijuana are back on the table. If smoking marijuana is no longer **illegal**, is there any other moral reason why Christians should avoid it? Saint Paul told us to obey the arbitrary laws of our nation (speed limits in school zones) for the common good.[51]

"Let every soul be subject to higher powers: for there is no power but from God: and those that are, are ordained of God." (Romans 13:1).

It used to be that pastors and youth ministers could tell teenagers, "It's illegal. Respect the law." That was not the most forceful argument, but at least it was something. Now, if you live in Colorado or Washington, that argument falls flat.[52]

Dr. Taylor Marshall writes:

> Marijuana (*Cannabis sativa, Cannabis indica, Cannabis ruderalis*) is not sinful in itself. (<u>Stay with me. Don't stop reading</u>). God created marijuana. It is an herb with medicinal purposes. When God created the herbs of creation, He remarked that they were all good, cannabis included. Now according to Saint Thomas Aquinas, a thing can be essentially good but used wrongly. Lead is essentially good. However, if I poison your water with lead, that's not good. If I shoot a pointed lead projectile (bullet) into your

chest, that's not good...So our argument about marijuana cannot center on the fact that "God created it, so it's morally okay."[53]

Question 29:

But God made all plants and he said "It is good." Well, marijuana is a plant that God made so, isn't it good?

Answer:

Plants are not all equal or healthy. Hemlock is a plant. God made hemlock but it will kill you; ask Socrates. Poison ivy is good; but I would not use it for camouflage, or body oil, or as an herb. Nightshade is a plant. Nightshade is good; however, it is poisonous. Would it be okay to put some Nightshade in a children's vitamin supplement? I don't think so! The Poppy is a good flower; the morphine we extract, used appropriately, is good. However, morphine used addictively is bad. Don't swallow the false mantra of the Woodstock sixties, they say, "Don't panic; it's organic." That's a half-truth. Some plants are not good or healthy as I have just demonstrated. God made marijuana and plants in general so that we could appreciate their aesthetic beauty and the wonders of nature. God didn't make marijuana with the specific intent of using it to numb our senses and shrink our brains (cf. Question and Answer #16). Pot has mind-altering properties. It's classified as a drug so when one uses marijuana for the specific purpose of getting "high", this is a sin denounced by the Catechism and the Holy Bible.

The Book of Enoch also describes how fallen angels taught humans how to utilize plants and cut roots to tap into their psychedelic compounds and to elicit metaphysical experiences and cast spells. Steven Bancarz says: "If transpersonal mystical experiences coming alongside the use of drugs cannot be called 'pharmakeia' (which means 'magik' with 'drugs'), I don't know what can. This is literally what the word means."[54]

If the government says it's legal; it is okay, isn't it?

Answer:

<u>Legal does not equal moral</u>. It was also legal to own slaves. It's legal to kill a baby in a mother's womb. It's legal to have a doctor kill you (euthanasia). It's legal for two men to get married. It's legal to produce pornography. These are some things that are legal unto man but an abomination unto God. Legalizing marijuana will not change the fact that it is not good for you and can cause spiritual, emotional and even physical problems. Don't forget: some laws are bad (like the examples I provided); however, laws that prevent bad things are good laws. "There are two ways to be fooled. One is to believe what isn't true; the other is to refuse to believe what is true" (Søren Kierkegaard).[55] The Bible weighs in on this question.

- 1 Corinthians 6:12 (RSV) "All things are lawful for me, but not all things are helpful. All things are lawful for me, but I will not be enslaved by anything." *Mind-altering drugs are addictive and enslave you to sin.*

- 1 Corinthians 10:23 (RSV) "All things are lawful, but not all things are helpful. All things are lawful but not all things build up." *Though smoking pot may be lawful, will it help you become holier? Will it make your prayer life better and draw you closer to God? Of course NOT!*

- 1 Corinthians 8:9 (NAB) "Only take care lest this liberty of yours somehow become a stumbling block to the weak." *If you're an adult, does smoking dope around your spouse and kids provide a bad example? Of course, it does, it makes you look like a hedonist that needs to live with an altered mind, has no self-discipline and no desire to master your disordered passions or do penance and practice mortification.*

Who is behind the major push for marijuana legalization?

Answer:

Billionaire George Soros is behind the major push for marijuana legalization. Hungarian-American billionaire and philanthropist George Soros is no stranger when it comes to throwing around money, but the former hedge fund manager is making headlines over some major donations he's made to help legalize marijuana. Advocacy groups are leading the campaign to crush marijuana prohibition from coast-to-coast, and 83-year-old Soros is helping line the pockets of those making that push.[56]

Reuters News reported on Wednesday, July 25, 2016 that Kelly Riddell at *The Washington Times* pulled back the curtain to reveal details about some of the roles that Soros has played in the pro-weed debate and helped explain how the billionaire's many foundations are fighting the war against pot prohibition. "*Through a network of nonprofit groups, Mr. Soros has spent at least $80 million on the legalization effort since 1994, when he diverted a portion of his foundation's funds to organizations exploring alternative drug policies, according to tax filings.*" The Soros-affiliated Foundation to Promote an Open Society donates roughly $4 million annually to the Drug Policy Alliance. This Alliance is a nonprofit group that describes itself as the nation's leading organization promoting drug policies that are grounded in science, compassion, health and human rights. Records obtained by the *Washington Times* also reveal that Soros cuts other substantial checks annually to the American Civil Liberties Union, "*which in turn funds* *marijuana legalization efforts,*" as well as the Marijuana Policy Project which funds state ballot measures.[57]

What about medical marijuana as a true painkiller?

Answer:

Dr. Taylor Marshall states in his article, "Is Marijuana Sinful for Christians":

> If you're going to pull a bullet from my arm and we have no painkillers, I'm getting drunk. And, that's okay. The same goes for the medicinal use of cocaine, opium, codeine, and marijuana. Of course, there must be a true medicinal cause. I don't think that "having a headache" or "anxiety" or "depression" is a just cause for smoking marijuana. I'll leave the details to the medical experts.

Medical marijuana would fall under the precept of...

Proverbs 31:6 "Give beer to those who are perishing, wine to those who are in anguish." There are times when alcohol or others drugs are allowed for a greater good. However, I don't think that Snoop Dogg's prescription for smoking weed every day while sipping on gin and juice meet the medicinal criteria. Any substance that inhibits rational functionality should not be indulged.[58]

Dr Vince Fortanasce (brain surgeon) says: "people tout that this CBD or cannabidiol has medicinal value. However, after you are no longer under the influence and you're sober, your sensitivity to pain increases. You can extract the CBD from marijuana but it's very expensive and we have drugs much less expensive that helps decrease your pain."[59]

How have the people of Colorado been impacted since they legalized medical marijuana in 2009 and recreational marijuana in 2012?

Answer:

Here are *7 Harmful Side Effects Pot Legalization Has Caused in Colorado* by Charles "Cully" Stimson, a leading expert in national security, homeland security, crime control, immigration and drug policy at The Heritage Foundation's Center for Legal and Judicial Studies and the Center for National Defense. The new report by the Rocky Mountain High Intensity Drug Trafficking Area entitled "The Legalization of Marijuana in Colorado: The Impact," states that the impact of legalized marijuana in Colorado has resulted in:

1. The majority of DUI drug arrests involve marijuana and 25 to 40 percent were marijuana alone.

2. In 2012, 10.47 percent of Colorado youth ages 12 to 17 were considered current marijuana users compared to 7.55 percent nationally. Colorado ranked fourth in the nation, and was 39 percent higher than the national average.

3. Drug-related student suspensions/expulsions increased 32 percent from school years 2008-09 through 2012-13; the vast majority was for marijuana violations.

4. In 2012, 26.81 percent of college age students were

considered current marijuana users compared to 18.89 percent nationally, which ranks Colorado third in the nation and 42 percent above the national average.

5. In 2013, 48.4 percent of Denver adult arrestees tested positive for marijuana, which is a 16 percent increase from 2008.

6. From 2011 through 2013, there was a 57 percent increase in marijuana-related emergency room visits.

7. Hospitalizations related to marijuana have increased 82 percent since 2008.

Pot is big business, and the push to legalize is really all about profit, despite inconvenient facts. Drug policy should be based on hard science and reliable data. In addition, the data coming out of Colorado points to one and only one conclusion: the legalization of marijuana in the state is terrible public policy.[60]

Who has more propensity to smoke marijuana and use other illegal drugs?

Answer:

Liberals are five times more likely than conservatives to use marijuana and cocaine.[61]

What does federal law say about marijuana?

Answer:

We are a society and nation governed under the rule of law and using illegal drugs violates the laws of our society.

> Marijuana is properly categorized under Schedule I of the Controlled Substances Act (CSA), 21 U.S.C. § 801, et seq. The clear weight of the currently available evidence supports this classification, including evidence that smoked marijuana has a high potential for abuse, has no accepted medicinal value in treatment in the United States, and evidence that there is a general lack of accepted safety for its use even under medical supervision.[62]

Despite recently approved laws in Washington and Colorado, marijuana remains an illegal narcotic under federal law.[63]

Question 36:

Is marijuana addictive?

Answer:

Marijuana is the number one addiction of 65% of teens that are in drug rehabilitation. Marijuana is a gateway drug to cocaine and methamphetamine (meth). Marijuana harms the lungs faster than smoking cigarettes. So, what's good about legalizing marijuana? Nothing! Legalization of marijuana means it could be sold in grocery stores. There will be skyrocketing usage of marijuana amongst teens and young people. We will see an increase in drugged driving on streets and freeways. People will have the right to get high while on the job. There will be higher insurance premiums as addictions soar. Marijuana operatives will buy thousands of acres of farmland.

Here is some straight talk. Marijuana legalization means messed up minds, messed up lives, messed up families and an even worse society. Is this the kind of culture you want? Don't buy the lie.[64] Contrary to common belief, marijuana can be addictive. Research suggests that 30 percent of users may develop some degree of problem use, which can lead to dependence and in severe cases takes the form of addiction.[65]

Question 37:

Is marijuana a gateway drug?

Answer:

According to Nora Volkow, M.D., Director of the National Institute on Drug Abuse reports:

> Some research suggests that marijuana use is likely to come before use of other drugs. Marijuana use is also linked to addiction to other substances, including nicotine. In addition, animal studies show that the THC in marijuana makes other drugs more pleasurable to the brain.[66] All forms of marijuana are mind-altering psychoactive drugs; they all contain THC (tetrahydrocannabinol), the main active chemical in marijuana. There are about 400 chemicals in a marijuana plant but THC is the one that affects the brain the most.[67] The marijuana used today is 25 times stronger than the marijuana used in the 1960's.[68]
>
> The amount of THC in marijuana has been increasing steadily over the past few decades. For a new user, this may mean exposure to higher THC levels with a greater chance of a harmful reaction. Higher THC levels may explain the rise in emergency room visits involving marijuana use. The popularity of edibles also increases the chance of users having harmful reactions. Edibles take longer to digest and produce a high. Therefore, people may consume more to feel the effects faster, leading to dangerous results.[69]

What is the percentage of inmates who committed crimes while under the influence?

Answer:

85% of inmates who are locked up in jail committed their crimes under the influence of drugs or alcohol or both.[70] Once they are sober, many of them wish they did not commit the crime and they all say that if they were sober they would not have done what they did.

Drugs deaden your senses and your moral conscience. Therefore, under the influence of drugs or alcohol or both you will do things and take risk that you would not normally take. How can you remember the 10 commandments, which is the eternal moral law, and have a clear understanding of "right" and "wrong" if you are under the influence? It's impossible. Marijuana use makes you a fuzzy thinking moral relativist.

Does the drug culture have the approval from the Hollywood stars and political elites?

Answer:

A 20-year study on marijuana reports the following:

> Celebrities and campaigners…claimed cannabis should be legalized. Prominent supporters of decriminalization in the United States have included actor Woody Harrelson, rapper Snoop Dogg and singer-songwriter Willie Nelson. Robert Downey Jr. participated in an AARP "Smoke-In" to support marijuana legalization in 2005…President Obama notoriously admitted to smoking cannabis as a youngster and told *New Yorker* magazine: "I don't think it is more dangerous than alcohol"…Jack Nicholson told the *Daily Mail* in 2011 that he still occasionally smokes marijuana, adding, "I don't tend to say this publicly, but we can see it's a curative thing." When asked, former president Bill Clinton said: "I experimented with marijuana a time or two." While promoting *Savages* in 2012, director Oliver Stone told the *Associated Press*, "[Legalization] can be done legally, safely, healthy, and it can be taxed and the government can pay for education and stuff like that. Also, you can save a fortune by not putting kids in jail."[71] On a side note, did you know that well over 500 actors, entertainers, and professional athletes have killed themselves through drug overdose in the last 50 years?[72]

Proverbs 14:12 (RSV) "There is a way which seems right to a man, but its end is the way to death."

Can you give me a common sense reason why I should not smoke marijuana and use illegal drugs?

Answer:

The body is God's perfect creation. Being well and sober is not a disease. Drugs are supposed to be taken as prescribed by a doctor when the body is sick and not functioning well. I only take drugs that are prescribed by a doctor who has studied medicine for about ten years and is certified and accredited by the State board of Physicians. I am not going to take drugs from Larry the loser, Danny the doper, Willie the weed-fiend, Manuel the marijuano, or Tommy the toker who is a high school dropout and is as intelligent as a box of rocks. Drug abuse is a crutch for the weak and a cop-out for cowards.

Are there any long-term studies that say habitual use of marijuana is harmful?

Answer:

A definitive 20-year study into the effects of long-term cannabis use has demolished the argument that the drug is safe. Cannabis is highly addictive, causes mental health problems and opens the door to hard drugs, the study found. The paper (published October 2014) by Professor Wayne Hall, a drugs advisor to the World Health Organization, builds a compelling case against those who deny the devastation cannabis wrecks on the brain.

Professor Hall found:

- One in six teenagers who regularly smoke the drug become dependent on it.

- Cannabis doubles the risk of developing psychotic disorders, including schizophrenia

- Cannabis users do worse at school. Heavy use in adolescence appears to impair intellectual development.

- One in ten adults who regularly smoke the drug become dependent on it and those who use it are more likely to go on to use harder drugs.

- Driving after smoking cannabis doubles the risk of a car crash, a risk which increases substantially if the driver has also had a drink.

    —   Smoking it while pregnant reduces the baby's birth weight.

Widespread: Teenagers and young adults are now as likely to take cannabis as they are to smoke cigarettes. Regular use, especially among teens, leads to long-term mental health problems and addiction. Professor Hall, a professor of addiction policy at King's College London, dismissed the views of those who say that cannabis is harmless. "If cannabis is not addictive then neither is heroin or alcohol," he said. "It is often harder to get people who are dependent on cannabis through withdrawal than for heroin – we just don't know how to do it."[73]

Those who try to stop taking cannabis often suffer anxiety, insomnia, appetite disturbance and depression, he found. Even after treatment, less than half can stay off the drug for six months. However, his main finding is that regular use, especially among teenagers, leads to long-term mental health problems and addiction. "The important point I am trying to make is that people can get into difficulties with cannabis use, particularly if they get into daily use over a longer period," he said. "There is no doubt that heavy users experience a withdrawal syndrome as with alcohol and heroin."[74]

David Raynes, of the National Drug Prevention Alliance, added: "There is no case for legalization and we hope that this puts an end to the matter. The two main parties agree that cannabis needs to remain illegal – we hope the Liberal Democrats see this research and re-examine their policies."[75]

Can you smoke marijuana, practice your Catholic faith and still be in the state of grace?

Answer:

Smoking marijuana, drug abuse and alcoholism is a serious and all too common problem today. The fact that it is rampant particularly among our youth makes the problem especially tragic. Whenever any drugs are abused, that begins the seed of death to any system of religious faith. Health programs, chemical substitutes, treatment techniques may free you from drug enslavement momentarily, but they cannot free you from the eternal slavery of sin. Only Jesus Christ, who died and rose again (1 Corinthians 15:3-4) can set you FREE from SIN.

Romans 6:17 (RSV) "But thanks be to God that you were once <u>slaves of sin</u>...have become obedient from the heart... and having been <u>set free from sin</u>."

Romans 8:2 (RSV) "For the law of the spirit of life in Christ Jesus has <u>set me free</u>, stand fast therefore, and do not submit again to a yoke of slavery."

Galatians 5:1 (RSV) "<u>For Freedom</u> Christ has <u>set us free</u>; stand fast therefore, and do not submit again to a <u>yoke of slavery</u>."

Here are the facts, drugs will leave you senseless, alcohol will leave you mindless but Jesus won't leave you regardless.

Can I become holy and saintly while smoking marijuana every day?

Answer:

Basic Catholic Moral Philosophy is "Do good and avoid evil."[76] Sobriety leads to > Virtue leads to > Holiness leads to > being a Saint in Heaven. Fr. Donald Calloway (a former drug addict) says "sobriety is a fruit of holiness."[77]

Does using illegal drugs, getting drunk and smoking pot affect your body?

Answer:

Yes, this is why so many people who become intoxicated on drugs, alcohol and or both end up on their knees in front of the porcelain god (i.e., the toilet) calling, "RALPH, RALPH." And boy, oh boy, does he come with a vengeance. The reason the body reacts so violently is because the body has been poisoned and the body is violently expelling the poisons that have been put into the body. Think about how people make a FOOL of themselves and regret things that they did and said while under the influence. The next day people lament and live with the regrets of the absolutely stupid things they committed while intoxicated. If you know that you are poisoning your body with drugs and/or alcohol and you have had several violent bouts on your knees in front of the toilet god, than your body is telling you to STOP. "The definition of insanity is doing the same thing over and over again and expecting different results!"[78]

What motivates drug dealers and what is the profile of drug users?

Answer:

Drug dealers are secular humanists and ideologically moral relativists who are motivated by greed. 1 Timothy 6:10 (RSV) describes them well, "the love of money is the root of all evils, it is through this craving that some have wandered away from faith." They are blinded by Satan. This verse describes them as well. 2 Corinthians 4:4 (NAB) "in whose case the god of this age has blinded the minds of the unbelievers so that they might not see the light of the gospel…"

Drug dealers and drug users are people who are secular humanists (live only for this world), moral relativists (there is NO objective truth), are generally weak-minded followers who are unmotivated by anything virtuous and suffer from boredom (idol time is the devil's workshop). Other drug users are in some kind of emotional, mental or psychological pain that stems from living in a state of constant mortal sin and NOT having a relationship with God. Drug users and drug dealers, because of their "wickedness, they suppress the truth" (cf. Romans 1:18) about God, His commandments and a life of moral virtue.

How does marijuana affect a user's life?

Answer:

Compared to nonusers, heavy marijuana users more often report the following:

— lower life satisfaction

— poorer mental health

— poorer physical health

— more relationship problems

Users also report less academic and career success. For example, marijuana use is linked to a higher likelihood of dropping out of school. It is also linked to more job absences, accidents, and injuries.[79]

Should Marijuana still be Taboo? How much THC is in that candy?

Answer:

Here are *7 reasons Why Marijuana should still be Taboo* given by Kathleen M. Berchelmann, M.D. Dr. Berchelmann is an Assistant Professor of Pediatrics at Washington University School of Medicine in St. Louis, a practicing Catholic and mother of five young children.

> My patients now recognize marijuana as a drug—a medical drug, that is. They tell their parents how it helps with depression and anxiety. And, I tell them I believe them. Marijuana probably does help them feel better. I also tell them we have other drugs to treat depression, anxiety, and pain, drugs that are better regulated and have risk profiles that are better understood, drugs with standard concentrations and doses. Nicotine, too, is a stimulant that can improve ADHD symptoms, but we don't recommend smoking as an ADHD treatment. We have better drugs for that, too. Recreational marijuana is losing its taboo identity now that it is legal in… sixteen states plus the District of Columbia have decriminalized possession of marijuana for personal use. I spent a summer in college doing cannabinoid research at the NIH, trying to understand the effects of marijuana in the brain…and its recreational use should still be taboo. Here's why:

1. **Is it synthetic?** A patient came into my ER hallucinating with tales of a very bad trip. He showed me his "marijuana," a bunch of leaves rolled into a joint. Then his drug screen came back negative. His was synthetic marijuana, a bunch of herbs sprayed with some unknown chemical. Synthetic marijuana often contains laboratory-manufactured chemicals that have the same effect as THC, the psychoactive ingredient in marijuana. But sometimes the product is actually laced with bath salts or other street drugs. I never really know what my patients have taken, which makes it hard for me to treat them.[80] Marijuana is not always what it seems, it can be laced with substances such as PCP, formaldehyde, or codeine cough syrup without your knowledge. "Blunts" are hollowed out cigars filled with marijuana, sometimes have crack cocaine.[81]

2. **How much THC is in that candy?** My four-year-old saw a brownie at a beach bake-sale and started begging me to buy it for him. The guy selling it looked me directly in the eyes and shook his head. I knew what he meant. Marijuana brownies, cookies, and jolly-rancher-like hard candies are common now. The problem is that you just don't know how much THC is in the treats. Some contain much higher concentrations than one joint, and who can eat only one cookie? The result is an overdose effect that can land people in the ER. Dr. Dan Hehir, an ER physician at Telluride Medical Center in Colorado, recounts <u>stories</u> of recreational

marijuana overdoses, especially in marijuana baked goods and candies.[82]

3. **Infertility:** Marijuana use reduces fertility in both men and women (no, marijuana is not a form of birth control). Anandamide is an "endogenous cannabinoid," a THC-like chemical that is naturally occurring in all of our bodies. Anandamide also helps human conception, giving signals to sperm to "hyper activate," or swim faster so they can penetrate the egg. (Anandamide is also in chocolate, perhaps one reason people often use the words "sex" and "chocolate" in the same sentence). Using marijuana sends signals to sperm to hyper activate too early, so they are all burned out before they ever reach the egg (*pun intended*). Marijuana use is also known to reduce the volume of sperm production. If women use marijuana, the THC is in their cervical fluids, also causing hyper activation of sperm and reducing the likelihood of conception.[83]

4. **Impaired Memory:** What was that? That's right, marijuana use impairs memory, a critical skill for academic success (marriage, too). Most of the time memory loss is subtle, just enough to cause a drop in school grades, but occasionally memory loss can be profound. A <u>case report</u> published last month (July 2014) describes a patient with marijuana-induced transient global amnesia.[84]

5. **Paranoia:** Marijuana can cause paranoia, especially in patients who have underlying mental illness. In a <u>study</u> published in July,

2014, intravenous THC was administered to 121 patients. The authors write, "THC significantly increased paranoia, negative affect, anxiety, worry, depression, negative thoughts about the self, and a range of anomalous experiences, and reduced working memory capacity."[85]

6. **Thrush:** or an <u>oral yeast infection</u>, can result from chronic marijuana smoking. There's a reason why some people call thrush "trench-mouth." A white film grows over the inside of your mouth and tongue.[86]

7. We don't really understand most of the **risks of marijuana:** This is perhaps the biggest problem with Marijuana – it's hard to study. Would you take a drug that is poorly researched? Research on marijuana is difficult because it is illegal in most states. There are possible associations with some forms of cancer, but because most marijuana users are also tobacco users it is difficult to determine the effects of the marijuana alone. There seems to be <u>an association with lung disease</u>, especially among people who smoke marijuana long term. Its addictive nature is perhaps most controversial. The bottom line is we don't understand this drug as we do most pharmaceuticals.[87]

Taboo or not, my patients take marijuana because they are desperate. Desperate to dull the pains of stress, anxiety, depression, and the hardships of life. Legalization of recreational marijuana is not the solution to these ills.[88]

If drug users and addicts have no free will, are they predetermined to be drug abusers?

Answer:

Drug addiction is a choice. Is there anyone of us who has never resorted to excuses about his circumstances when he has done wrong or made a bad decision? It is a universal human tendency. In Britain, an entire class of persons has been created who not only indulges in this tendency, but also makes it their entire world outlook – and does so with official encouragement. Let's take an example the case of heroin addicts. In the 1950's, heroin addiction in Britain was confined to a very small number of people, principally in Bohemian circles. It has since become a mass phenomenon, the numbers of addicts have increased perhaps 2000 fold, to something like 250,000 to 300,000…Heroin addiction has been presented by officialdom as a bona fide disease that strikes people like, shall we say, rheumatoid arthritis. In the United States, the National Institute on Drug Abuse defines addiction quite boldly as a chronic relapsing brain disease *and nothing else.*[89]

I hesitate to say it, but this seems to me straightforwardly a lie, told to willing dupes in order to raise funds from the federal government. Nevertheless, the impression has been assiduously created and peddled among addicts that they are helpless victims of something that is beyond their control, which means they need the technical assistance of what amounts to a substantial bureaucratic apparatus in order to overcome it. Research has shown medical treatment is not necessary for heroin addicts to abandon their habit and that many thousands do so without any medical intervention whatsoever. In other words, the entire basis upon which heroin addiction is treated as if it is something that happens to people, rather than something that people *do* are false, and easily shown to be false.[90]

I have taken the example of heroin addiction as emblematic of what, with some trepidation, I may call the dialectical relationship between the worldview of those at the bottom of society and the complementary worldview of what one might call the Salvationist bureaucracy of the government. In the old Soviet Union, there was a joke in which the workers would say to the party bosses, "We pretend to work and you pretend to pay us." In the case of the heroin addicts, they might say, "We pretend to be ill, and you pretend to cure us." This is surely a very curious but destructive state of mind and one that some politicians have unfortunately made it their interest to promote by promising secular salvation…"[91]

My son told me that he is obsessed with marijuana just like I am obsessed with the Catholic religion. How do I respond to him?

Answer:

There are good kinds of obsessions like being obsessed with zeal in spreading the gospel, as Paul was (Romans 15:19). but demonic obsession compels people to do harmful or imprudent things, they believe lies, are often trapped in cults, lose all perspective, and are contaminated with deceiving spirits (cf. 1 Timothy 4:1). The free functioning of the will is thus impaired at this point by alcohol, drugs, the influence of fortune telling, astrology, etc. The victim may be obsessed with pornography, jealousy, lack of forgiveness, hatred, child abuse, sexual perversions, etc. To break strongholds like these much prayer and fasting is needed.[92]

Question 50:

What does the person need to overcome drug addiction?

Answer:

We need to embrace a life of "<u>Virtue</u>," which means: moral excellence, right living; goodness. Virtue is a good quality or feature such as purity, chastity, effectiveness. Virtue comes from the Latin word *virtus*, which means *manliness* or *virility – which often means a man's ability to impregnate a woman.*

CCC 1810 – Human virtues acquired by education, by deliberate acts and by a perseverance ever renewed in repeated efforts are purified and elevated by divine grace. With God's help, they forge character and give facility in the practice of the good. The virtuous man is happy to practice them.

CCC 1811 – It is not easy for man, wounded by sin, to maintain moral balance. Christ's gift of salvation offers us the grace necessary to persevere in the pursuit of the virtues. Everyone should always ask for this grace of light and strength, frequent the sacraments, cooperate with the Holy spirit, and follow his calls to love what is good and shun evil. *Ask yourself the question, "'Is using marijuana going to make you HOLIER?" I think you know the answer to that question.*

To overcome drug addiction we need to specifically practice the virtues of "prudence" and "temperance."

CCC 1806 – *Prudence* is the virtue that disposes practical reason to discern our true good in every circumstance and to choose the right means of achieving it: "the prudent man looks where he is going"... "Keep sane and sober for your prayers." Prudence is "right reason in action" says St. Thomas Aquinas, following Aristotle. It is not to be confused with timidity or fear, nor with duplicity or dissimulation. It is called *Auriga virtutum* (the charioteer of the virtues); <u>it guides the other virtues by setting rule and measure. It is prudence that immediately guides the judgment of conscience. The prudent man determines and directs his conduct in accordance with this judgment. With the help of this virtue we apply moral principles to particular cases without error and overcome doubts about the good to achieve and the evil to avoid.</u>

CCC 1809 – *Temperance* <u>is the moral virtue that moderates the attraction of pleasures and provides balance in the use of created goods. It ensures the will's mastery over instincts and keeps desires within the limits of what is honorable. The temperate person directs the sensitive appetites toward what is good and maintains a healthy discretion</u>: "Do not follow your inclination and strength, walking according to the desires of your heart." Temperance is often praised in the Old Testament: "Do not follow your base desires, but restrain your appetites." In the New Testament it is called "moderation" or "sobriety." We ought "to live sober upright and godly lives in this world." To live well is nothing other than to love God with all one's heart, with all one's soul and with all one's efforts; from this it comes that love is kept whole and uncorrupted (through temperance). No misfortune can disturb it (and this is fortitude). It obeys only [God] (and this is justice), and is careful in discerning things, so as not to be surprised by deceit or trickery (and this is prudence).

Finally, the best way to live a life of sobriety and overcome drug addiction is to have a God-centered mind, because only the God centered mind can cope without a cop-out with the challenges of life.

- Isaiah 26:3 (RSV) puts it this way: "Thou dost keep him in perfect peace, whose mind is stayed on thee, because he trusts in thee."

- 2 Chronicles 20:12 (RSV) "For we are powerless against this great multitude that is coming against us. We do not know what to do, but our eyes are upon thee."

- Psalm 123:2 (RSV) "Behold, as the eyes of the servants look to the hand of their master...so our eyes look to the LORD our God, till he have mercy upon us."

- Hebrews 12:2 (RSV) "looking to Jesus the pioneer and perfecter of our faith..."

- Jeremiah 29:11-13 (RSV) "For I know the plans I have for you, says the Lord, plans for your welfare and not for evil, to give you a future and a hope. Then you will call upon me and come and pray to me, and I will hear you. You will seek me and find me; when you seek me with all your heart."

I recommend that this final chapter be read in the presence of Jesus Christ, either before Him in the Blessed Sacrament or before Him in the Tabernacle, preferably on your knees. Every situation will be different according to your state in life and where you are in your formation. St. Paul reminds us that "now is the acceptable time; behold, now is the day of salvation" (cf. 2 Corinthians 6:2). We must work out our salvation with fear and trembling (cf. Philippians 2:12) and persevere in the spiritual battle. We are (by virtue of our Baptism and Confirmation) soldiers of Christ. We are called to obedience and to run the race according to the commandments otherwise we will not be crowned (cf. 2 Timothy 2:3-5).

Before we get into what your spiritual game plan can look like; it would be prudent to discuss the issue of psychologists, therapy and (or) psychiatrists. Are they necessary? If so, then how should one be selected? Let us begin with what the Church teaches as it relates to this subject.

Let me point out that under the Fifth Commandment, the *Catechism of the Catholic Church* declares the following:

1. Science and technology are precious resources when placed at the service of man and promote his integral development for the benefit of all. By themselves however, they cannot disclose the meaning and existence of human progress. Science and technology are ordered to man, from whom they take their origin and development; hence, they find in the person in his moral values

both evidence of their purpose and awareness of their limits.[93]

2. Science and technology by their very nature require unconditional respect for fundamental moral criteria. They must be at the service of the human person of his inalienable right, of his true and integral good, in conformity with the plan and the will of God.[94]

3. Scandal is an attitude or behavior which leads another to do evil. The person who gives scandal becomes his neighbor's tempter. He damages virtue and integrity; he may even draw his brother into spiritual death. Scandal is a grave offense if by deed or omission another is deliberately led into a grave offense. Scandal takes on a particular gravity by reason of the authority of those who cause it or the weakness of those who are scandalized. It prompted our Lord to utter this curse: "Whoever causes one of these little ones who believe in me to sin, it would be better for him to have a great millstone fastened round his neck and to be drowned in the depth of the sea"…Scandal is grave when given by those who by nature or office are obliged to teach and educate others. Jesus reproaches the scribes and Pharisees on this account: he likens them to wolves in sheep's clothing. Scandal can be provoked by laws or institutions, by fashion or opinion. Therefore, they are guilty of scandal who establish laws or social structures leading to the decline of morals and the corruption of religious practice, or to "social conditions that,

intentionally or not, make Christian conduct and obedience to the Commandments difficult and practically impossible." This is also true of business leaders who make rules encouraging fraud, teachers who provoke their children to anger, or manipulators of public opinion who turn it away from moral values.[95]

Let us remind ourselves that the Fifth Commandment is Thou Shall Not Kill (Murder). Any type of medical science should be ordered towards the well-being of man according to the will of God for the benefit of his (her) immortal soul. When modern psychology is not aimed towards man's end, which is to inherit the kingdom of God, then the psychologist, therapist, or psychiatrist could be causing grave scandal under the Fifth Commandment. It is fair to say that our priests should also understand the Church's teaching on this subject. This is important if one is seeking a spiritual director or regular confessor.

In his book, *Tracing Our Sins to Adam and Eve*, John Garcia (a former drug addict) states:

> In fact, my research has shown that nine out of ten people diagnosed with a mental health disorder as a result of their bad moral habits or sinfulness have actually been misdiagnosed. The proof is in the results found in one treatment center located in Des Moines, Iowa. This facility, (The Saint Gregory Retreat Center), was founded by two Catholics. They are getting incredible results with their methods of detox and treatment for those who are struggling with addictions.[96]

Herein lies the problem with medicating subjects

prior to the supernatural healing found in the Sacraments. This is the problem with modern psychology.

Our Lord and Savior Jesus Christ warned us about what would happen if we do not base our endeavors on Him and His Eternal Truth. Let me summarize; it will be "like a fool who built his house on sand. The rain came, and the winds blew and buffeted the house. And it collapsed and was completely ruined" (cf. Matthew 7:24-27). This applies especially to the science of modern psychology. Since it does not have a solid foundation in an authentic view of man, modern psychology is doomed to be "swept away" to the scrap of futility.[97]

I am in no way suggesting that there isn't a place for modern psychology or psychiatry in society. What I am pointing out is that there needs to be a cohesive method of selecting a psychologist or psychiatrist. These individuals who treat God's children need to be informed as it relates to man and his faculties. Here are some guidelines and recommendations[98] in selecting a psychologist or therapist:

1. The person you select must believe and understand the Doctrine of Original Sin and the consequences of the fall (meaning our concupiscence).

2. It is critical that this individual understand the healing power of Confession and the meaning of sanctifying grace, including the meaning of the

Real Presence in the Holy Eucharist.

3. This person must understand the spiritual battle as it relates to the demonic and what the fallen angels are permitted to do by God. It is important because of the three types of diabolical activity that affect man (possession, obsession, and oppression). The person you select should understand their limitations and defer to a trained priest when there is evidence of diabolical activity.

4. He (she) should have some training in Thomistic Philosophy (the writings of our Common and Angelic Doctor, Saint Thomas Aquinas). I highly recommend *An Introduction to the Science of Mental Health*, written by Fr. Chad Ripperger, FSSP, Ph.D. This book will give your director (the person who is treating you) a solid foundation in the understanding of man and his nature. This book should be read by every Catholic in the mental health field and priests who are treating the addicted.

5. Your selection must have a devotion to the Blessed Virgin Mary and the holy angels. Praying the rosary is a key component in helping God's children. Praying to each other's guardian angel in the treatment process will also benefit the individuals involved since angels can direct man's intellect to assent to the will of God.

I would suggest praying to your guardian angel in all things to help you make a good decision in your selection. I would note here that if you are taking medication as a result of your addiction(s), then my prudent recommendation would be to get two other opinions from trained Catholic Christian therapists who meet the criteria I mentioned above.

One of the best sources for developing your own game plan can be found in the *Daily Roman Missal* published by *Our Sunday Visitor*. The following section of this chapter was taken directly from the 2003 edition and modified respectively for this book.[99]

The first thing we should ask ourselves: "How can I be a really good Christian?" The first of your battles will be to remain in the state of grace and to avoid any mortal sin. And, then, because you want to love God above all things, you will also try not to commit any venial sins.

The practice of some acts of piety throughout the day will help you to have a divine contemplative life in the midst of the daily routine. The habitual performance of these acts also will be the foundation for growing in Christian virtues. Most important is to be consistent in your daily schedule, in your spiritual game plan, so that you will live as a child of God.

Practices—Daily

- Get up at a fixed time, as early as possible. Eight hours of sleep should be enough. More than this or less than seven hours of sleep is usually not healthy.

- Start your day with the Sign of the Cross and pray to your Guardian Angel, including praying morning prayers.

- Offer your day to God through the intercession of Our Lady.

- Work with order and intensity during the day as a way of serving our God. Set goals and establish priorities in order to develop a practical schedule. Sanctifying ordinary work is the goal of our life.

- Try to attend Mass, receiving Holy Communion as often as possible. This is the best sacrifice we can offer God. Prepare yourself for Mass by spending some time in prayer.

- Spend time in prayer before the Blessed Sacrament (15 minutes if possible).

- Pray the Angelus at noontime. (During Eastertime, say the Regina Caeli instead).

- Pray the Rosary—if possible, with your family—offering each decade for a specific intention.

- Do some spiritual reading. Start with the New Testament of the Bible or some well-known spiritual book. Ten to fifteen minutes is sufficient.

- Make a short examination of conscience at the end of the day before going to bed. Follow these steps. Humble yourself in the presence of God. Tell Him, "Lord, if You will, You can make me clean." Ask for light to acknowledge your defects and virtues and to see the dangers and opportunities of the day. Ask for repentance, amendment, and encouragement.

Practices–Weekly

- Center all activities around the Holy Mass on Sunday, the Lord's Day. It is also a family day for rest and spiritual growth.

- If you do not receive Holy Communion every day, receive at least on Sundays and holy days of obligation. Saturday is traditionally dedicated to the Blessed Virgin Mary. Honor her and say some special prayer, such as the Hail Holy Queen.

- If you have struggled with a particular vice for years, then frequenting the Sacrament of Confession will be very effective in your battles with the enemy or dealing with your *fomes peccati* or concupiscence. Read paragraphs 1426 and 1496 in the Catechism to better understand why this would be important. I would encourage frequenting this Sacrament at least once a week for the first year of your path back to spiritual wellness.

Practices–Monthly

- Go to Confession at least once a month. It is a Sacrament of joy. St. John Paul II said, "God is always the one Who is principally offended by sin — '*tibi soli peccaviii*' — against you alone have I sinned," and God alone can forgive." God does this through the ministry of the priest in the Sacrament of Reconciliation, which "is the ordinary way of obtaining forgiveness and remission of mortal sins committed after Baptism." "Every serious sin must always be stated, with its determining circumstance, in an individual confession."[100]

— Seek and follow the spiritual guidance of a wise, prudent and knowledgeable priest.

— Spend a few hours in recollection, best done before the Blessed Sacrament. Consider how you are directing your life toward God.

Practice–Yearly

— Spend two or three days each year in silence, speaking with God only. A few days of retreat are needed and necessary for the soul in the same way the body needs a vacation. It is a yearly opportunity for conversion.

— Always remain in the presence of God; be aware He is always close to you. Try to please Him in everything as a child tries to please his parents.

— Thank God for the graces He constantly gives you.

— Do everything for the love of God, this should be your motive and intention. Make Acts of Contrition and atonement for your sins and the sins of others.

— Try to live as you would like to die because we shall die as we have lived.

Devotions During the Week

Devotion is defined as "the disposition of will to do promptly what concerns the worship and service of God. Although devotion is primarily a disposition or attitude of the will, acts of the will that proceed from such disposition are also expressions of devotion...devotedness is ultimately rooted in a great love for God."[101]

Sunday: The Blessed Trinity
Attend Mass (Sunday is obligatory) and, if possible, receive Holy Communion. Cultivate in your heart a great zeal for the One and Triune God Mark your calendar for all Holy Days of Obligation.

Monday: The Souls in Purgatory
Pray for the souls of your relatives, Godparents, and friends.

Tuesday: Guardian Angels
Pray often to your Guardian Angel, asking for assistance.

Wednesday: Saint Joseph
Pray to Saint Joseph, so that you may obtain a good and holy death.

Thursday: The Holy Eucharist
Throughout the day, say many spiritual communions. Make a visit to the Blessed Sacrament.

Friday: The Passion and Death of Our Lord Jesus Christ
Using the Way of the Cross, meditate on the

passion and death of Our Lord.

Saturday: The Blessed Virgin Mary
Pray the Rosary or practice another Marian devotion.

Prayers against Temptation

Lord Jesus Christ, Who wast conducted as a criminal to the house of Annas, grant that I may never suffer myself to be led into sin by the temptations of the evil spirit or the evil suggestions of my fellow creatures, but that I may be securely guided by Thy divine Spirit in the perfect accomplishment of thy holy ordinances. Amen.

Come, O Holy Spirit, and destroy in me, by Thy sacred fire, every affection which cannot be referred to Thee or please Thee. Grant that I may be all Thine, that I may live and die ever true to Thee, my Love and my All. O Mary, my Advocate and Mother, help me by thy prayers. Amen.

Prayer to be Freed from Evil Habits

Give me, I beseech thee, O Holy Spirit, Giver of all good gifts, that powerful grace which converts the stony hearts of mortals into burning furnaces of love. By Thy grace, free my captive soul from the thralldom of every habit and concupiscence, to restore to it the holy liberty of the children of God. Give me to task how sweet it is to serve the Lord and crucify the flesh with its vices and concupiscence. Enlarge my heart that I may ever cheerfully run the way of Thy commandments until I reach the goal of my aspirations, the joys and bliss of Thy habitation in heaven. Amen.

Prayer to Overcome our Spiritual Enemies

Eternal Wisdom, come down so powerfully into my soul, that all my enemies may be driven out; all my crimes melted away; all my sins forgiven. Enlighten my understanding with the light of true faith; inflame my will with Thy sweet love; clear up my mind with Thy glad presence; and give virtue and perfection to all my powers. Watch over me especially at my death, that I may come to enjoy Thy beatific vision in eternal bliss. Amen.

Prayer to Overcome Evil Passions and to Become a Saint

Dear Jesus, in the Sacrament of the Altar, be forever thanked and praised. Lover, worthy of all celestial and terrestrial love! Who, out of infinite love for me, ungrateful sinner, didst assume our human nature, didst shed Thy Most Precious Blood in the cruel scourging, and didst expire on a shameful cross for our eternal welfare! Now, illumined with lively faith, with the outpouring of my whole being and the fervor of my heart, I humbly beseech Thee, through the infinite merits of Thy painful sufferings, to give me strength and courage to destroy every evil passion which sways my heart, to bless Thee in my greatest afflictions, to glorify Thee by the exact fulfilment of my duties, supremely to hate all sin, and thus to become a saint. Amen.

Invocation of the Entire Heavenly Court

O Glorious Queen of Heaven and Earth, Virgin Most Powerful, thou who have the power to crush the head of the ancient serpent with thy heel, come and exercise this power flowing from the grace of thine Immaculate Conception. Shield us under the mantle of thy purity and love, draw us into the sweet abode of thy heart and annihilate and render impotent the forces bent on destroying us. Come, Most sovereign Mistress of the Holy Angels and Mistress of the Most Holy Rosary, thou who from the very beginning hast received from God the power and the mission to crush the head of Satan. We humbly beseech thee, send forth thy holy legions, that under thy command and by thy power they may pursue the evil spirits, encounter them on every side, resist their bold attacks and drive them far from us, harming no one on the way, binding them immobile to the foot of the Cross to be judged and sentenced by Jesus Christ Thy Son so that he may dispose the forces of darkness, repel the attacks of the devil and free your son (daughter) N., from the strong hold the enemy has upon his (her) soul. St. Michael, summon the entire heavenly court to engage their forces in this fierce battle against the powers of hell. Come, O Prince of Heaven, with thy mighty sword and thrust into hell Satan and all the other evil spirits. O Guardian Angels, guide and protect us. Amen.

Binding Prayer to Blind the Demons

Most gracious Virgin Mary, thou who wouldst crush the head of the serpent, protect us from the vengeance of the evil one. We offer our prayers, supplications, sufferings and good works to you so that you may purify them, sanctify them and present them to thy Son as a perfect offering. May this offering be given so that the demons that influence us (or seek to influence us or name the person) do not know the source of their expulsion and blindness. Blind them so they know not our good works. Blind them so that they know not on whom to take vengeance. Blind them so that they may receive the just sentence for their works. Cover us with the Precious Blood of thy Son so that we may enjoy the protection which flows from His Passion and Death. We ask this through the same Christ Our Lord. Amen.

Memorare

Remember, O most gracious Virgin Mary, that never was it known that anyone who fled to thy protection, implored thy help, or sought thine intercession was left unaided. Inspired by this confidence, I fly unto thee O Virgin of Virgins, my mother, to thee do we come. Before thee we stand, sinful and sorrowful, O Mother of the Word Incarnate, despise not my petitions, but in thy mercy hear and answer me. Amen.

Anima Christi

Soul of Christ, sanctify me. Body of Christ, save me. Blood of Christ, inebriate me. Water from the side of Christ, wash me. Passion of Christ, strengthen me. Oh Good Jesus, hear me. Within your wounds, hide me. Separated from you let me never be, from the evil one, protect me. At the hour of my death, call me. And close to you keep me, that with your saints and angels I may praise you forever and ever – Amen.

Prayer Against Every Evil

Spirit of our God, Father, Son, and Holy Spirit, Most Holy Trinity, Immaculate Virgin Mary, Angels, Archangels, and Saints of heaven, descend upon me. Please purify me, Lord, mold me, fill me with Thyself, and use me. Banish all the forces of evil from me, destroy them vanquish them, so that I can be healthy and do Thy Holy Will. Banish from me all spells, witchcraft, black magic, malefice, ties, maledictions, and the evil eye; diabolic infestations, oppressions, possessions; all that is evil and sinful; jealousy, perfidy, envy; physical, psychological, moral, spiritual, diabolical ailments. Cast into hell all demons working these evils, that they may never again touch me or any other creature in the entire world. I command and bid all the powers who molest me by the power of God Almighty, in the Name of Jesus Christ our Savior, through the intercession of the Immaculate Virgin Mary, to leave me forever and to be consigned into the everlasting hell, where they will be bound by Saint Michael the Archangel, Saint Gabriel, Saint Raphael and our Guardian Angels, and where they will be crushed under the heel of the Immaculate Virgin Mary.[102]

Prayer for Inner Healing

Dear Lord Jesus, please come and heal my wounded and troubled heart. I beg you to heal the torments that are causing anxiety in my life. I beg you, in a particular way, to heal the underlying source of my sinfulness. I beg you to come into my life and heal the psychological harms that struck me in my childhood and from the injuries that have caused emotional pain throughout my life.

Lord Jesus, you know my burdens. I lay them on your Good Shepherd's Heart. I beseech you by the merits of the great open wound in your heart, to heal the small wounds that are in mine. Heal my memories, so that nothing that has happened to me will cause me to remain in pain and anguish, filled with anxiety.

Heal, O Lord, all those wounds that have been the cause of all the evil that is rooted in my life. I want to forgive all those who have offended me. Look to those inner sores that make me unable to forgive. You who came to forgive the afflicted of heart, please heal my wounded and troubled heart.

Heal, O Lord Jesus, all those intimate wounds that cause me physical illness. I offer you my heart. Accept it, Lord, purify it and give me the sentiments of your Divine Heart.

Heal me, O Lord, from the pain caused by the death of my loved ones. Grant me to regain peace and joy in the knowledge that you are the Resurrection and the Life. Make me an authentic witness of your resurrection, your victory over sin and death, and your loving presence among all men — Amen.[103]

Saint Patrick's Breastplate Prayer

I bind unto myself today
The strong Name of the Trinity,
By invocation of the same,
The Three in One and One in Three.

I bind this day to me forever.
By power of faith, Christ's incarnation;
His baptism in the Jordan River;
His death on Cross for my salvation;
His bursting from the spiced tomb;
His riding up the heavenly way;
His coming at the day of doom;
I bind unto myself today.

I bind unto myself the power
Of the great love of the Cherubim;
The sweet "well done" in judgment hour,
The service of the Seraphim,
Confessors' faith, Apostles' word,
The Patriarchs' prayers, the Prophets' scrolls,
All good deeds done unto the Lord,
And purity of virgin souls.

I bind unto myself today
The virtues of the starlit heaven,
The glorious sun's life-giving ray,
The whiteness of the moon at even,
The flashing of the lightning free,
The whirling wind's tempestuous shocks,
The stable earth, the deep salt sea,
Around the old eternal rocks.

I bind unto myself today
The power of God to hold and lead,

His eye to watch, His might to stay,
His ear to hearken to my need.
The wisdom of my God to teach,
His hand to guide, His shield to ward,
The word of God to give me speech,
His heavenly host to be my guard.

Against the demon snares of sin
The vice that gives temptation force,
The natural lusts that war within,
The hostile men that mark my course;
Or few or many, far or nigh,
In every place and in all hours,
Against their fierce hostility,
I bind to me these holy powers.

Against all Satan's spells and wiles,
Against false words of heresy,
Against the knowledge that defiles,
Against the heart's idolatry,
Against the wizard's evil craft,
Against the death wound and the burning,
The choking wave and the poisoned shaft,
Protect me, Christ, till Thy returning.

Christ be with me, Christ within me,
Christ behind me, Christ before me,
Christ beside me, Christ to win me,
Christ to comfort and restore me.
Christ beneath me, Christ above me,
Christ in quiet, Christ in danger,
Christ in hearts of all that love me,
Christ in mouth of friend and stranger.

I bind unto myself the Name,
The strong Name of the Trinity;
By invocation of the same.
The Three in One, and One in Three,
Of Whom all nature hath creation,
Eternal Father, Spirit, Word:
Praise to the Lord of my salvation,
Salvation is of Christ the Lord.

For Catholics in Fighting Drug and Alcohol Addiction:

– <u>Prevencion y Rescate</u> (Bilingual Catholic drug and alcohol ministry)

  1321 S. Mariposa Ave., L.A. (323) 496-0740. Founder – William Portillo.

– <u>Our Lady of Hope Community</u> (Catholic drug and alcoholic ministry)

  5985 S.R. 16
  St Augustine FL 32092
  (940) 829-0404
  http://www.hopereborn.org/about/

– <u>St Gregory Retreat Center</u>

  http://www.stgregoryctr.com/Home.aspx, Iowa
  (866) 216-6314

on the topic of marijuana:

Go to the National Institute on Drugs Website:
http://www.drugabuse.gov/infofacts/marijuana.
html
and
http://www.drugabuse.gov/NIDAHome.html.
There is a plethora of information on the harmful
effects of marijuana use from a scientific medical
perspective.

www.MarijuanaHarmsFamilies.com
Our friends at SaveCalifornia.com have created
a beautiful and useful website to inform and
activate concerned Californians.

http://teens.drugabuse.gov/
Great Resource for teens.

Endnotes

1. "What is Marijuana?" *DrugFacts: Marijuana*. National Institute on Drug Abuse, Mar. 2016. Web. 20 July 2016.

2. Larson, Bob. *Satanism: The Seduction of America's Youth*. Nashville: T. Nelson, 1989. Print.

3. "What is Marijuana?" *DrugFacts: Marijuana*. National Institute on Drug Abuse, Mar. 2016. Web. 20 July 2016.

4. Ibid.

5. Vine, W. E., Merrill F. Unger, and William White. *Vine's Complete Expository Dictionary of Old and New Testament Words: With Topical Index*. Nashville: T. Nelson, 1996. Print.

6. Bob Larson Ministries. *Marijuana*. Denver: Bob Larson Ministries, 1988. Print.

7. Amorth, Gabriele. *An Exorcist Tells His Story*. San Francisco, CA: Ignatius, 1990. Print.

8. Vine, W. E., Merrill F. Unger, and William White. *Vine's Complete Expository Dictionary of Old and New Testament Words: With Topical Index*. Nashville: T. Nelson, 1996. Print.

9. "Is Marijuana Sinful for Christians? A Thomistic Analysis - Taylor Marshall." *Taylor Marshall*. N.p., 05 Aug. 2013. Web. 20 July 2016.

10. Ibid.

11. Ibid.

12. McLeod, Jeffrey. "How God Reveals Himself in Memory." Web log post. *Catholic Stand*. Little Vatican Media, 23 Sept. 2014. Web.

13. Gallegos, Juan Jose, Fr. "Spanish Exorcist Reveals Satan's Favorite Sin." *ChurchPOP*. Catholic News Agency, 2015. Web. 20 July 2016.

14. White, Hilary. "Westminster Exorcist Says Promiscuity Can Lead to Demonic Possession." Web log post. *LifeSiteNews.com*. N.p., 15 Aug. 2008. Web.

15. "Drugs, Drugs All Around: Sometimes Invaluable, at Other Times they may Reflect Back on 'Pharmakeia'." *Drugs and the Occult*. Spirit Daily, n.d. Web. 22 July 2016.

16. Larson, Bob. *Satanism: The Seduction of America's Youth*. Nashville, TN: T. Nelson, 1989. Print.

17. Ibid.

18. "Drugs, Drugs All Around: Sometimes Invaluable, at Other Times they may Reflect Back on 'Pharmakeia'." *Drugs and the Occult*. Spirit Daily, n.d. Web. 22 July 2016

19. Ibid.

20. Ibid.

21. Ibid.

22. Ibid.

23. Burnham, Jim. *Beginning Apologetics: How to Explain and Defend the Catholic Church, #4*. Farmington, NM: San Juan Catholic Seminars, 1993. Print.

24. Rey, Joseph M., and Christopher C. Tennant. "Cannabis and Mental Health: More Evidence Establishes Clear Link between Use of Cannabis and Psychiatric Illness." *National Center for Biotechnology Information*. BMJ: British Medical Journal, 23 Nov. 2002. Web. 23 July 2016.

25. Ibid.

26. Owen, Jonathan. "Cannabis: An Apology." *Health News* (17 Mar. 2007): n. p. *Independent*. Independent Digital News & Media, 17 Mar. 2007. Web.

27. "The Definition of Psychosis." *Dictionary.com*. Houghton Mifflin Company, 2005. Web. 23 July 2016.

28. Owen, Jonathan. "Cannabis: An Apology." *Health News* (17 Mar. 2007): n. p. *Independent*. Independent Digital News & Media, 17 Mar. 2007. Web.

29. Ibid.

30. Spencer, Ben, and Wills Robinson. "The Terrible Truth about Cannabis:

Expert's Devastating 20-year Study Finally Demolishes Claims That Smoking Pot Is Harmless." *DailyMail.com*. Associated Newspapers, Ltd, 7 Oct. 2014. Web.

31. Warner, Jennifer. "Marijuana Use May Shrink the Brain." *Brain & Nervous System Health Center*. WebMD, 2 June 2008. Web. 23 July 2016.

32. Ibid.

33. "What is Marijuana?" *DrugFacts: Marijuana*. National Institute on Drug Abuse, Mar. 2016. Web. 24 July 2016.

34. Ibid.

35. Ibid.

36. Ibid.

37. Fickewirth, John. "Marijuana Use among Teens on the Rise." *Association for Los Angeles Deputy Sheriffs Dispatcher* Mar. 2013: 25. Print.

38. Ibid.

39. Nortz, Basil. *Deliver Us from Evil*. Detroit: Canons Regular of the Holy Cross, 2000. Print.

40. Spencer, Ben, and Wills Robinson. "The Terrible Truth about Cannabis: Expert's Devastating 20-year Study Finally Demolishes Claims That Smoking Pot Is Harmless." *DailyMail.com*. Associated Newspapers, Ltd, 7 Oct. 2014. Web.

41. *Catechism of the Catholic Church: With Modifications from the Editio Typica*. New York: Doubleday, 1997. Print.

42. "Samuel Smiles." *Wikiquote*. Wikimedia Foundation, 22 Sept. 2015. Web. 26 July 2016.

43. Chacon, Frank, and Jim Burnham. *Beginning Apologetics*. Farmington, NM: San Juan Catholic Seminars, 1993. Print.

44. Ibid.

45. Stewart, David J. "Do What Thou Wilt Shall Be the Whole of the Law." *Jesus Is Savior.com*. N.p., July 2012. Web. 26 July 2016.

46. "Aleister Crowley." *Wikipedia*. Wikimedia Foundation, 21 July 2016. Web. 25 July 2016.

47. Larson, Bob. *Satanism: The Seduction of America's Youth*. Nashville: T. Nelson, 1989. Print.

48. Ibid.

49. Ibid.

50. Ibid.

51. "Is Marijuana Sinful for Christians? A Thomistic Analysis - Taylor Marshall." *Taylor Marshall*. N.p., 05 Aug. 2013. Web. 25 July 2016.

52. Ibid.

53. Ibid.

54. Showalter, Brandon. "New Ager-Turned-Christian Steven Bancarz Exposes Connection Between Psychedelic Drugs and Witchcraft." *The Christian Post*, Christian Post, 26 Sept. 2017, www.christianpost.com/news/new-ager-turned-christian-steven-bancarz-exposes-connection-between-psychedelic-drugs-and-witchcraft-200623/.

55. "Søren Kierkegaard Quotes." Review. Web log post. *Goodreads*. Goodreads, Inc., 2016. Web. 29 July 2016.

56. "Billionaire George Soros Behind Major Push For Marijuana Legalization | Marijuana Debate." *Before It's News*. Before It's News Inc., 2016. Web. 25 July 2016.

57. Ibid.

58. "Is Marijuana Sinful for Christians? A Thomistic Analysis - Taylor Marshall." *Taylor Marshall*. N.p., 05 Aug. 2013. Web. 25 July 2016.

59. Radio Interview on Immaculate Heart Catholic Radio 11-2-16; 11am to 12-noon hosted by "the Terry & Jesse Show".

60. Stimson, Cully. "7 Harmful Side Effects Pot Legalization Has Caused in Colorado." *The Daily Signal*. The Heritage Foundation, 20 Aug. 2014. Web. 26 July 2016.

61. Meyers, Jim. "Are Liberals Bigger Drug Users?" *Newsmax*. Newsmax Media, 16 June 2008. Web. 26 July 2016.

62. *The DEA Position on Marijuana*. [Washington, D.C.]: Department of Justice: Drug Enforcement Administration, Apr. 2013. PDF.

63. "Billionaire George Soros Behind Major Push For Marijuana Legalization | Marijuana Debate." *Before It's News*. Before It's News Inc., 2016. Web. 25 July 2016.

64. "Colorado Children Hurt by Legal Pot." *Marijuana Harms Families. com*. Campaign for Children and Families, 1 Jan. 2014. Web. 26 July 2016.

65. "What is Marijuana?" *DrugFacts: Marijuana*. National Institute on Drug Abuse, Mar. 2016. Web. 26 July 2016.

66. Volkow, Nora D. "Letter From the Director." *Marijuana*. National Institute on Drug Abuse (NIDA), Mar. 2016. Web. 26 July 2016.

67. "What Is Marijuana?" *Marijuana: Facts Parents Need to Know*. KidsSource Online, 25 July 2000. Web. 26 July 2016.

68. *Marijuana: Your Child and Drugs*. Elk Grove Village, Il: American Academy of Pediatrics, Mar. 1996. PDF.

69. "What is Marijuana?" *DrugFacts: Marijuana*. National Institute on Drug Abuse, Mar. 2016. Web. 20 July 2016.

70. "Facts About Prison and Drug Use." *Home Health Testing*. Home Health Testing, 28 June 2010. Web. 26 July 2016.

71. Spencer, Ben, and Wills Robinson. "The Terrible Truth about Cannabis: Expert's Devastating 20-year Study Finally Demolishes Claims That Smoking Pot Is Harmless." *DailyMail.com*. Associated Newspapers, Ltd, 7 Oct. 2014. Web.

72. "List of Drug-related Deaths." *Wikipedia*. Wikimedia Foundation, 7 July 2016. Web. 26 July 2016.

73. Spencer, Ben, and Wills Robinson. "The Terrible Truth about Cannabis: Expert's Devastating 20-year Study Finally Demolishes Claims That Smoking Pot Is Harmless." *DailyMail.com*. Associated Newspapers, Ltd, 7 Oct. 2014. Web.

74. Ibid.

75. Ibid.

76. *Catechism of the Catholic Church: With Modifications from the Editio Typica*. Paragraph 1776-1777. New York: Doubleday, 1997. Print.

77. Fr. Donald, Calloway, MIC. *No Turning Back*. Lighthouse Catholic Media, n.d. CD.

78. Moncur, Michael. "The Quotations Page: Quote from Albert Einstein." *The Quotations Page*. QuotationsPage.com, 2015. Web. 29 July 2016.

79. "What is Marijuana?" *DrugFacts: Marijuana*. National Institute on Drug Abuse, Mar. 2016. Web. 20 July 2016.

80. Berchelmann, Kathleen M. "7 Reasons Why Marijuana Should Still Be Taboo." *Aleteia*. Aleteia SAS, 28 Aug. 2014. Web. 26 July 2016.

81. *Marijuana Facts: Why Is Smoking Marijuana Is Not a Good Idea*. Rockville, MD: Substance Abuse and Mental Health Services Administration Health Information Network, n.d. PDF.

82. Berchelmann, Kathleen M. "7 Reasons Why Marijuana Should Still Be Taboo." *Aleteia*. Aleteia SAS, 28 Aug. 2014. Web. 26 July 2016.

83. Ibid.

84. Ibid.

85. Ibid.

86. Ibid.

87. Ibid.

88. Ibid.

89. Daniels, Anthony. "The Worldview That Makes the Underclass." *Imprimus*. May-June 2014: 3+. Print.

90. Ibid.

91. Ibid.

92. Hampsch, John H. *How to "Raze" Hell : Strategies for Spiritual Warfare*. N.p.: Queen, 2000. Print.

93. Ibid, 2294.

94. Ibid, 2284, 2285, 2286.

95. Ibid.

96. Garcia, John H. *Tracing Our Sins to Adam & Eve*. West Covina: St. Joseph Communications, 2011. Print.

97. Ibid.

98. Ibid.

99. Socías, James, ed. *Daily Roman Missal: Sunday and Weekday Masses for Proper of Seasons, Proper of Saints, Common Masses, Ritual Masses, Masses for Various Needs and Occasions, Votive Masses, Masses for the Dead: Complete with Readings in One Volume, including Devotions and Prayers*. Chicago, IL: Midwest Theological Forum, 2003. Print.

100. Paul, Jean. *Reconciliatio Et Paenitentia*. Rome: n.p., 1984. Print.

101. Hardon, John A. *Pocket Catholic Dictionary*. New York: Doubleday, 1979. Print.

102. Paul, Jean. *Reconciliatio Et Paenitentia*. Rome: n.p., 1984. Print.

103. Ibid.